MAR 30 2009

STEP INTO HISTORY

CONQUEST!

Can You Build a Roman City?

By Julia Bruce

Illustrated by Peter Dennis

Enslow Elementary

an imprint of

Enslow Publishers, Inc.

40 Industrial Road
Box 398
Berkeley Heights, NJ 07922
USA

http://www.enslow.com

Enslow Elementary, an imprint of Enslow Publishers, Inc.
Enslow Elementary® is a registered trademark of Enslow Publishers, Inc.

US edition published in 2009 by Enslow Publishers, Inc.
First published in 2007 by Orpheus Books Ltd.,
6 Church Green, Witney, Oxfordshire, OX28 4AW, England

Created and produced by
Julia Bruce, Rachel Coombs, Nicholas Harris, Sarah Hartley, and Erica Simms, Orpheus Books Ltd.
Text Julia Bruce
Illustrated by Peter Dennis *(Linda Rogers Associates)*
Consultant Philip Wilkinson

Library of Congress Cataloging-in-Publication Data
Bruce, Julia.
  Conquest!: can you build a Roman city? / Julia Bruce.
    p. cm. — (Step Into History)
  Includes bibliographical references and index.
  Summary: "Readers will learn how the Romans extended their empire and built cities, roads, and aqueducts." — Provided by publisher.
  ISBN-13: 978-0-7660-3478-5
  ISBN-10: 0-7660-3478-X
  1. Rome—Army—Juvenile literature. 2. Building—Rome—Juvenile literature. 3. Cities and towns, Ancient—Rome—Juvenile literature. 4. Rome—History—Empire, 30 B.C. - 476 A.D.—Juvenile literature.
I. Title
U35.B765 2009
355.00937—dc22

                                                    2008019762

To Our Readers: We have done our best to make sure all Internet Addresses in this book were active and appropriate when we went to press. However, the author and the publisher have no control over and assume no liability for the material available on those Internet sites or on other Web sites they may link to. Any comments or suggestions can be sent by e-mail to comments@enslow.com or to the address on the back cover.

Printed and bound in China.

10 9 8 7 6 5 4 3 2 1

Contents

The Challenge

It is the first century AD. The Roman Empire is getting bigger by the day. Rome has been successful in conquering new lands because its army is extremely well-organized, its soldiers are well-trained, and its generals are great leaders. Now Rome wants to add even more land to its Empire, to increase its wealth. It especially wants to find new sources of copper, tin, iron, and other precious metals. It also needs food—and slaves. Rome requires you, a general in the Roman army, to help achieve this goal.

The challenge is to conquer a barbarian region—one that currently lies outside the Roman Empire—and make it part of the Empire. If you are successful, the rewards will be great.

Victorious army leaders gain control over the lands they conquer. As a governor you will be very rich and powerful. But you will also be expected to govern wisely. You must keep the peace, collect fair taxes, and build new towns for people to live in.

There are many things to know when planning a conquest and building a new Roman province. How is the army organized and what is the best way to attack the barbarians? How can you keep things inside the fort running smoothly from day to day? How do you build good roads and towns? Can you defeat the barbarians and make your province rich for Rome?

How the Army Is Organized

In the first century AD, the Roman army is the most professional, organized, well-trained, and best-equipped fighting force in the western world. It is divided into legions. Legions are made up of smaller groups called cohorts, centuries, and contubernia.

A contubernium is a group of eight soldiers. They will live, train, and fight together during their time as legionaries, or member of a legion. Ten contubernia, or 80 men, make up a century. This is the smallest fighting unit in a legion. It is commanded by a centurion. Six centuries make up a standard cohort.

In each legion there are nine standard cohorts. There is also one special cohort, called the prima cohort. This is made up of 10 centuries, or 800 men.

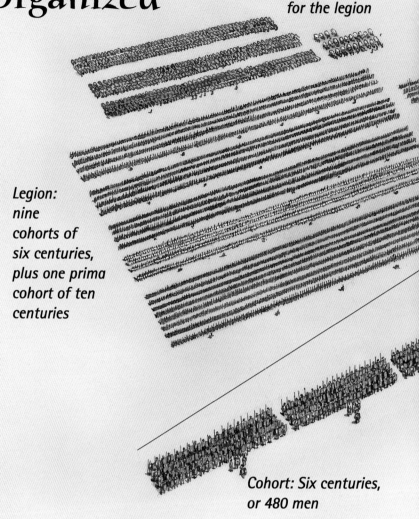

Legion: nine cohorts of six centuries, plus one prima cohort of ten centuries

Cohort: Six centuries, or 480 men

Legionary

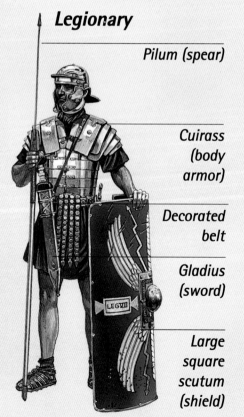

Pilum (spear)

Cuirass (body armor)

Decorated belt

Gladius (sword)

Large square scutum (shield)

The legionary is a basic footsoldier. Legionaries must be Roman citizens, at least 5 1/2 feet tall, and physically fit with good eyesight. Wages are good, and the army pays for their food, clothing, and weapons.

Signifer

Signum

Animal skin

Chain mail

Small round shield

Hand grip

Sandals

The signifer carries the century's standard or flag. He also organizes the soldiers' "burial club." Legionaries pay a small amount of their salary each week into this fund to pay for the cost of their funeral.

Cavalry: 120 men

Century: Ten contubernia,
or 80 men

There are about 120 cavalry soldiers in the legion. They often come from wealthy families. The cavalry soldier carries a sword, a one-handed fighting spear, and several smaller spears for throwing. These are called javelins.

Fighting spear

Saddle designed to grip rider securely

Bedroll

Aquilifer

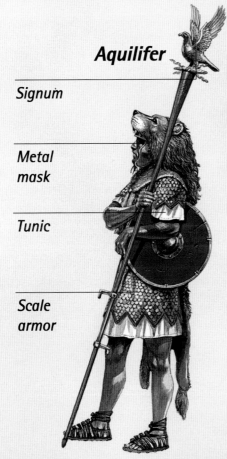

Signum

Metal mask

Tunic

Scale armor

The aquilifer carries the standard of the legion. This is a gold or silver eagle. Standard bearers have an important duty not to lose the symbol of the legion in battle. This would bring disgrace to the whole legion.

Centurion

Plume to show rank

Helmet

Leather harness with medals called phalerae (FAY-ler-aye)

Vine stick

Shin guards

The centurion commands the century. They are paid well. They wear silver armor. Their plumed, or feathered, helmet shows their rank. They carry a crooked stick made of vine to help discipline soldiers.

Marching Camp

Aim to march about 18 miles a day to get your army to its destination. Any more and you risk tiring out your troops. Each day, as evening approaches, send out scouts to find and mark a good site to make camp. Remember, it will take about two hours to set up camp. It's best to finish setting up while it is still light.

Your troops will carry most of the things they need. They should be well trained in what they have to do. Make sure the layout of the camp is the same each night. This makes setting up easier. It also means the troops can always find their way around after dark.

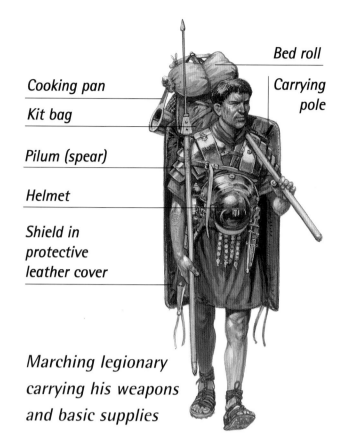

Bed roll

Cooking pan

Carrying pole

Kit bag

Pilum (spear)

Helmet

Shield in protective leather cover

Marching legionary carrying his weapons and basic supplies

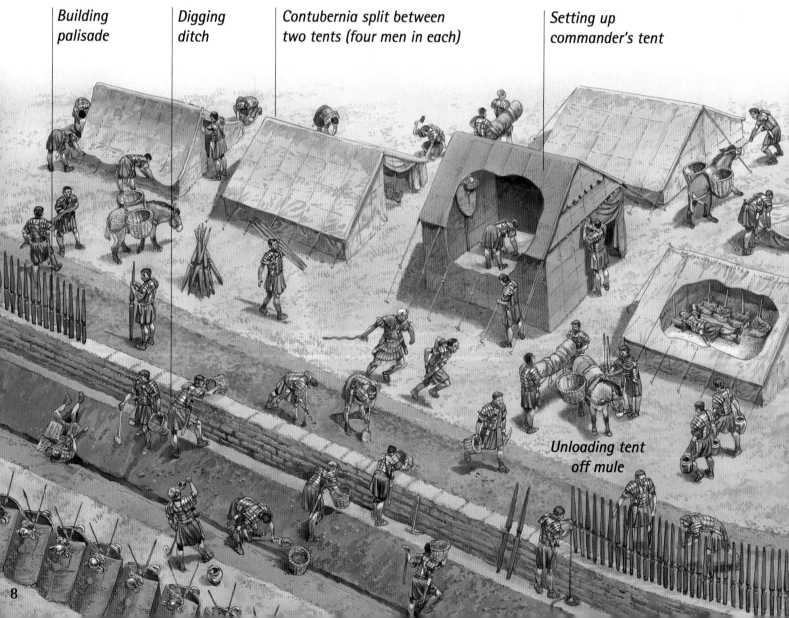

Building palisade

Digging ditch

Contubernia split between two tents (four men in each)

Setting up commander's tent

Unloading tent off mule

Rearguard Auxiliaries   Legionaries   Baggage   Generals   Camp builders   Legionaries   Scouts
cavalry   and standards

Legionaries have to carry all their own supplies and equipment. These include rations of food and water, weapons, a shield, a cooking pan, razor, and comb. Mules carry the heavy leather tents. An army column includes scouts to go ahead of the main army, standard bearers, camp builders, legionaries, generals, baggage mules, cooks, cavalry, and auxiliaries (extra soldiers).

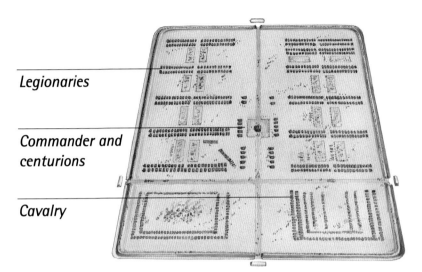

Legionaries

Commander and
centurions

Cavalry

**Plan of marching camp for
one legion**

Putting up
leather tents

Supply wagon

Removing dirt

Sharpened
stake bundles

Shields
and
weapons
ready in
case of
attack

If you plan to camp for a few days, secure the camp by digging a defensive ditch around it. Build ramparts, or protective walls, made from dirt. Set a palisade, or fence of sharpened stakes, on top of the ramparts. For overnight camps, create a barrier by placing bundles of sharpened stakes around the camp edge to deter intruders. Post one century to stand guard overnight. Check supplies and get the men busy cooking. Your troops need to be well fed to march and fight.

Into Battle!

The barbarians are not going to give up their land easily. They have raised a large army to fight you. This is no time to hold back. You must be ruthless in your battle tactics.

Enemy cavalry charging

Commander issuing orders

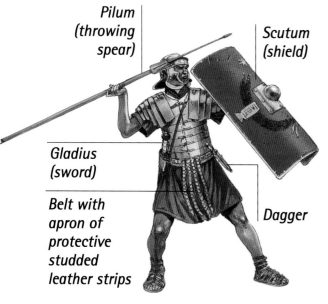

Pilum (throwing spear)

Scutum (shield)

Gladius (sword)

Belt with apron of protective studded leather strips

Dagger

Sword fighting is for combat at close range. The shield protects the body so that only the fighting arm is exposed. The troops keep their weapons in their right hand and their shield in their left. There isn't room on the battlefield to have some of the troops fighting the other way around. Launch javelins at the enemy over the troops' heads.

Cuirass (body armor)

Tunic

Sandals

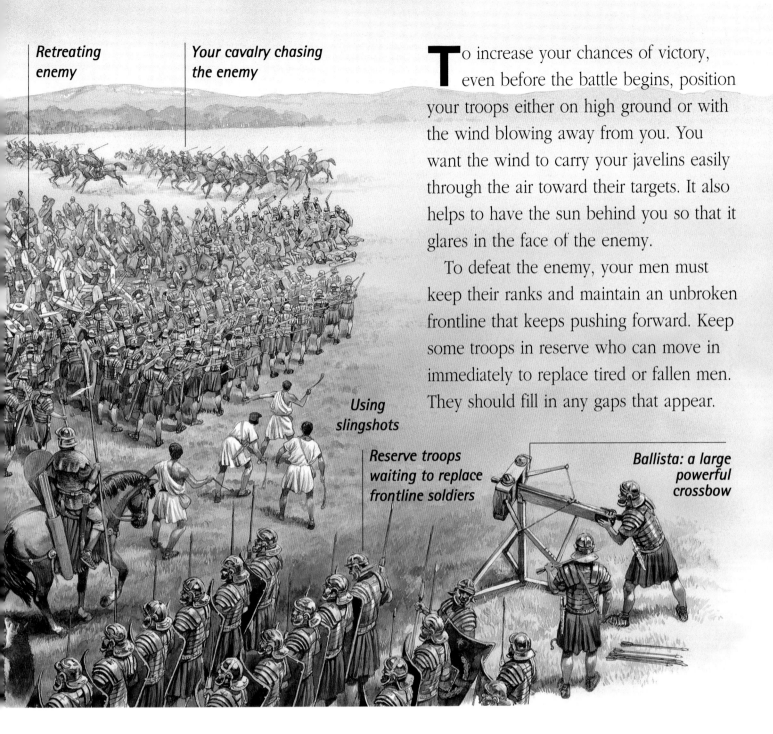

Your cavalry chasing the enemy

To increase your chances of victory, even before the battle begins, position your troops either on high ground or with the wind blowing away from you. You want the wind to carry your javelins easily through the air toward their targets. It also helps to have the sun behind you so that it glares in the face of the enemy.

To defeat the enemy, your men must keep their ranks and maintain an unbroken frontline that keeps pushing forward. Keep some troops in reserve who can move in immediately to replace tired or fallen men. They should fill in any gaps that appear.

Using slingshots

Reserve troops waiting to replace frontline soldiers

Ballista: a large powerful crossbow

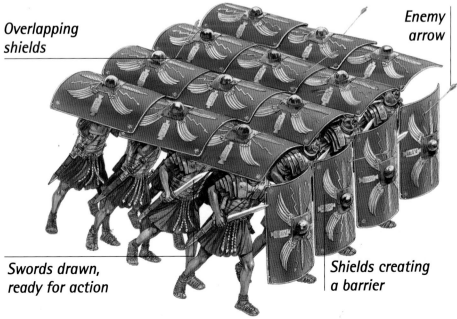

Overlapping shields

Enemy arrow

Swords drawn, ready for action

Shields creating a barrier

This is the testudo, which means tortoise. The troops march in close formation, overlapping their shields both over their heads and in front of them. This forms an almost unbreakable barrier that will protect them from arrows and spears as they advance toward the enemy. The testudo is very useful during battle to get close to the target.

Building a Fort

After the battle has been won, it is essential to establish your army's claim to the land as soon as possible. Give your soldiers a chance to celebrate their victory—and mourn the deaths of their comrades. But it is urgent that you build a fort to protect the area.

Give the order to start building the very next day. It is likely that enemy forces will regroup and attempt to win back their lands. A delay in making the fort could result in heavy losses in this hostile land. The fort will be a permanent base for around 500 troops.

Camp

Shields, helmets, and weapons ready

Leveling ground

Surveyors using a groma to mark out right angles

Carrying away timber

1 Your first task is to choose a good site for the fort. This should be on high ground to force the enemy to climb a slope to make an attack. Have the ground leveled and cleared of trees and bushes. Your surveyors should stake out the layout of the main roads and buildings.

Site of fort

KEY TO PLAN

- Barracks
- Headquarters
- Granary
- Workshops
- Commanding officer

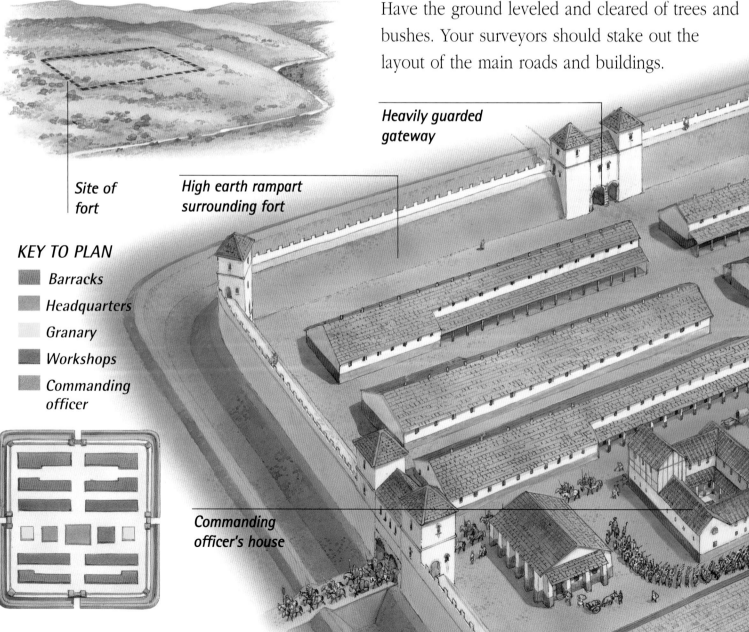

Heavily guarded gateway

High earth rampart surrounding fort

Commanding officer's house

2 Next, construct the fort's defenses. Command a group of your troops to dig the ditches that will become the fort's walls. Strip dirt from the whole area. The rubble and earth should be used to build the ramparts. Order other troops to collect timber for the buildings. The carpenters should then start cutting the timber to shape.

Plastering

Section of wall made of timbers and wattle

Carpenter working at a trestle

3 The walls of the buildings should be built in sections. These will be put into place later. Each section has a wooden "skeleton" filled in with wattle (interwoven sticks) and daub (rough plaster). The walls are attached to thick posts and given a coating of smooth plaster. They are painted to look like blocks of stone.

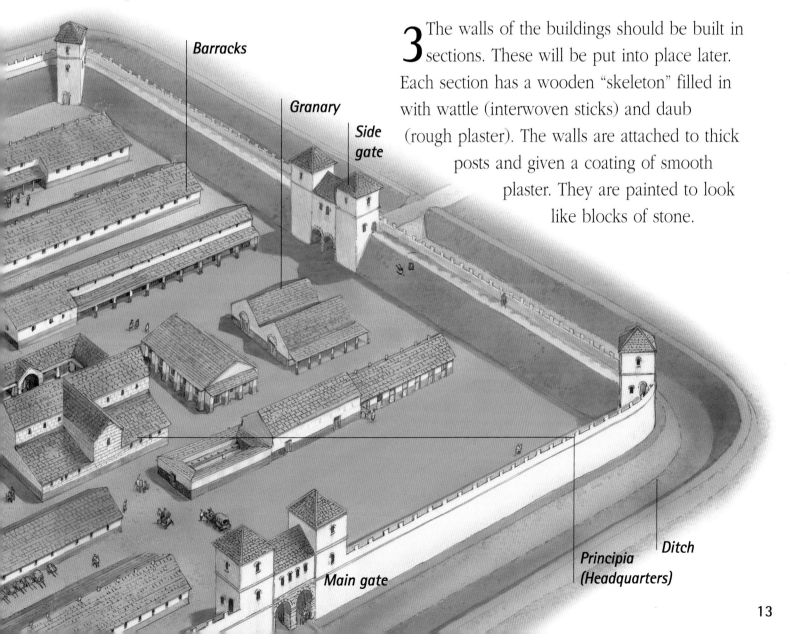

Barracks

Granary

Side gate

Main gate

Principia (Headquarters)

Ditch

Inside the Fort

Auxiliaries

Barracks

Centurion

Principia
(Headquarters)

Commander's
house

Officers'
wives
and
children

Barbarian
prisoner

Stables

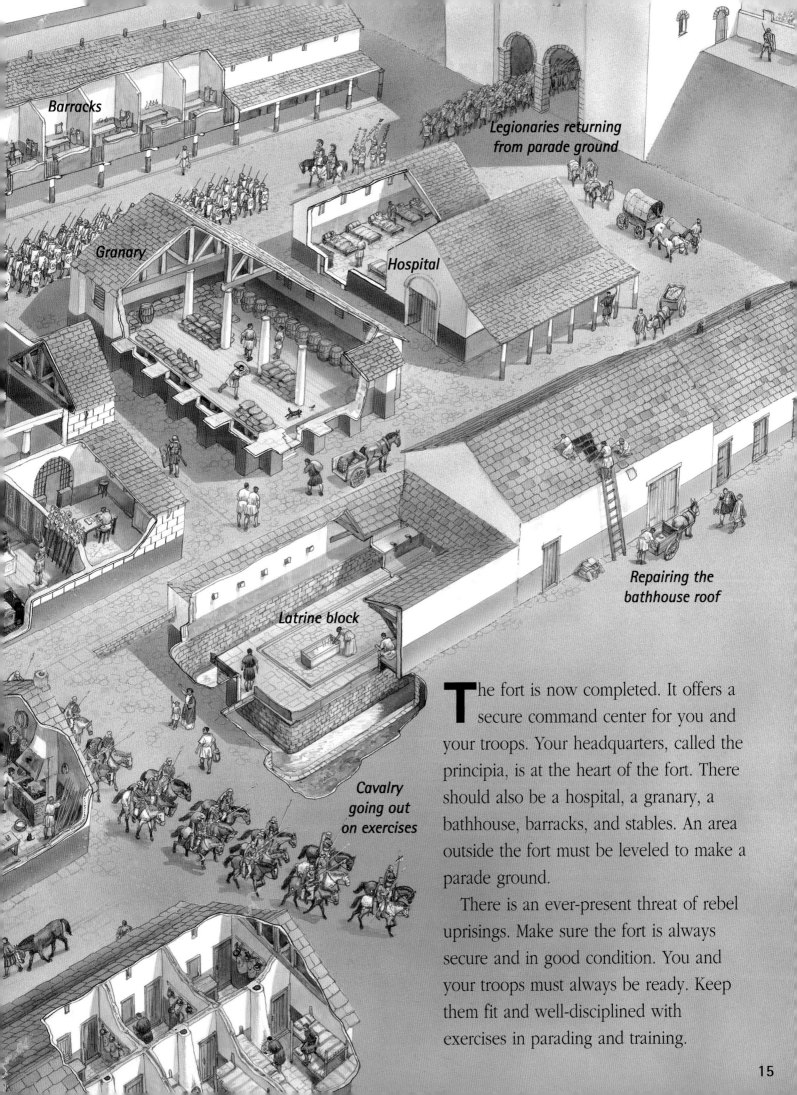

Barracks

Granary

Hospital

Legionaries returning
from parade ground

Repairing the
bathhouse roof

Latrine block

Cavalry
going out
on exercises

The fort is now completed. It offers a secure command center for you and your troops. Your headquarters, called the principia, is at the heart of the fort. There should also be a hospital, a granary, a bathhouse, barracks, and stables. An area outside the fort must be leveled to make a parade ground.

There is an ever-present threat of rebel uprisings. Make sure the fort is always secure and in good condition. You and your troops must always be ready. Keep them fit and well-disciplined with exercises in parading and training.

Daily Life in the Fort

The troops must be kept busy while in camp. There is plenty to be done. The troops need to stay fit, disciplined, and focused. There is a mix of experienced soldiers and new recruits in the legion. The recruits especially need to use their time practicing their fighting skills.

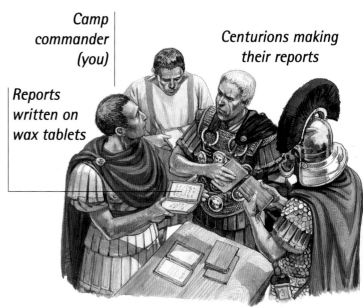

Camp commander (you)

Reports written on wax tablets

Centurions making their reports

Legionaries lined up for inspection

Centurion scolding a legionary

The day starts with the morning report. All centurions must give you, the camp commander, a written account listing how many men are available for work and what tasks have already been assigned. You then discuss the jobs for the day and divide them up between the centuries. Finally, you tell the centurions the day's password. This is to keep the fort secure. Without the password, soldiers who leave the camp will not be allowed back in.

Line up your men for inspection on the parade ground before the centurions give them their tasks for the day. Your centurions should punish any legionary who is not properly dressed or equipped. Legionaries must train every day.

Make sure new recruits are taught fighting skills and spend several hours a day in practice. They should use wooden swords and practice moves against a training stake until they have learned to control their weapons. They could easily hurt each other if they used real weapons at this stage.

Practicing against a training stake

Training stake

Your army is still fighting against small bands of barbarians in the province. Injured troops are coming back to the fort daily. There is only basic medical aid in the camp hospital. Wounds are stitched up or cauterized, which means they are burned to seal them. Broken bones are set in a splint. The surgeon might need to amputate, or cut off, badly injured limbs.

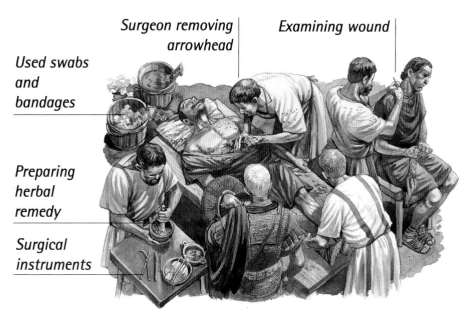

Surgeon removing arrowhead

Examining wound

Used swabs and bandages

Preparing herbal remedy

Surgical instruments

Your legionaries are not permitted to have wives or families. It would distract them from their duties to Rome. However, you and your centurions are allowed this privilege.

Keeping order in the fort is important. Soldiers must obey orders instantly. Disobedience and laziness must not be tolerated. A centurion will beat any soldier who steps out of line. If a soldier deserts his post, he could be executed if he is caught. The commander will decide. Such punishments will help keep other troops under control.

Centurion's plumed helmet shows his rank

Stick used to beat soldiers

Training officer

Recruits using training weapons

Cavalry at javelin practice

Ruling the Land

Waste no time in bringing this barbarian land under Roman control as a new province. You might find the local population against you at first, so be strict and firm. But remember that one thing that has made Rome's governors successful is their tolerance of local customs.

Keep order, but let the people continue to follow their own ways and religions. Find out how much wealth the people in the land have. That's how you decide how much tax they should pay to Rome. Introduce Roman coins to make trade with the rest of the Empire easier.

Governor receiving tax | Centurion | Barbarian leader

Gold aureus

Bronze sestertius

Silver denarius

Rome demands that all provinces pay tax, a part of their wealth to pay public expenses. Some of this will go back to Rome. You can also use some to fund your building program here. Do not over-tax and do not take bribes. You must be seen to be fair to gain trust and respect. Taxes may be taken in the form of crops, goods, or money.

Plastering a new building

Begin a building program at once. Over time, the fort will expand into a real town. If you are near the coast, you might need to build a port. Money from taxes can be used to construct public buildings like bathhouses, a basilica (town hall), granaries, and an amphitheater (pronounced AM-fi-thee-ter). Streets should be laid out in a grid pattern and paved so that they don't turn into mud in the rain. Building a water and sewage system is another important part of bringing the Roman way of life to your province.

It is important that you can get supplies easily and safely. That's why you should build good roads before anything else. If the local people are still hostile toward you, they might attack supply trains. Make sure these supply trains are always guarded by armed soldiers. In time you will probably want to start importing valuable luxury items like wine and glass from other parts of the Empire.

Finished pots ready to go in kiln

Kiln

Potter at work

| Oxen | Armed guard | Supply convoy | Newly built road |

You will need craftsmen, such as carpenters, leatherworkers, smiths, and potters to provide the town with goods and services. Some came here with you from Rome, but you should encourage local people to set up their own businesses in the town.

Stepping stones across the street

Public water supply

Shops

Building the basilica (town hall)

Carriage

Public bathhouse

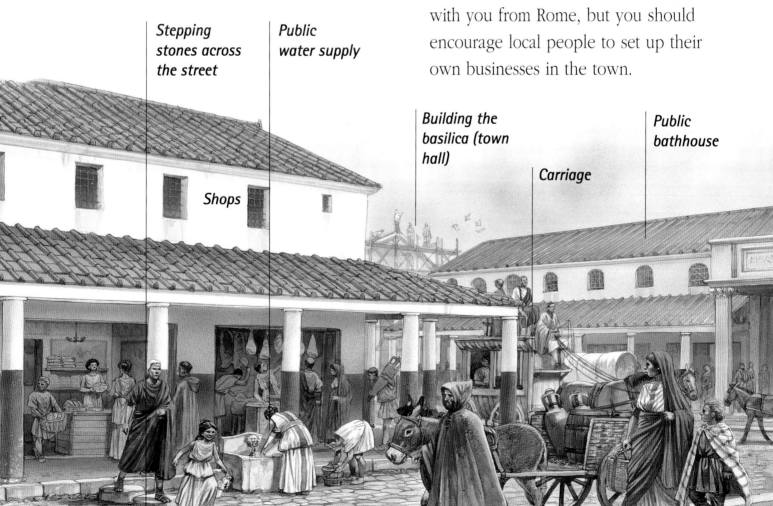

Building an Aqueduct

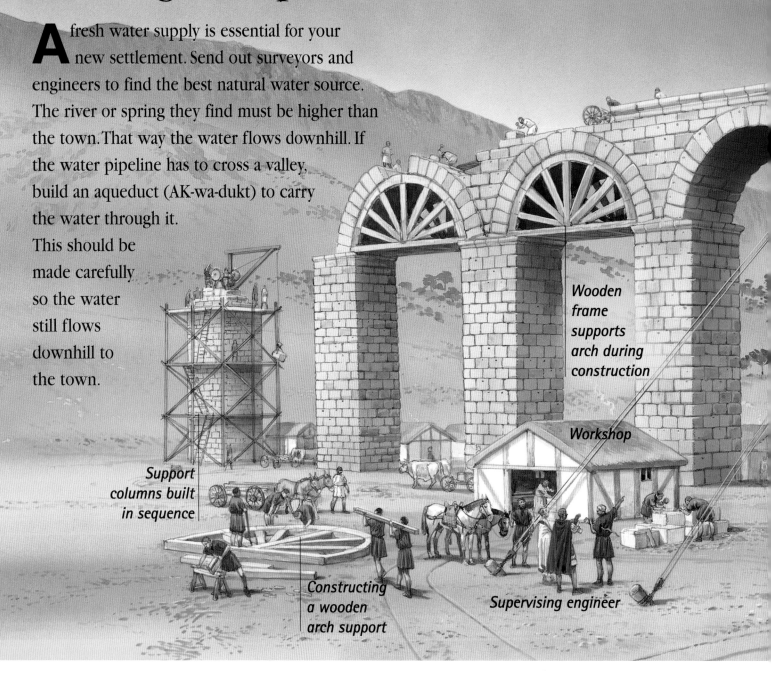

A fresh water supply is essential for your new settlement. Send out surveyors and engineers to find the best natural water source. The river or spring they find must be higher than the town. That way the water flows downhill. If the water pipeline has to cross a valley, build an aqueduct (AK-wa-dukt) to carry the water through it. This should be made carefully so the water still flows downhill to the town.

Wooden frame supports arch during construction

Workshop

Support columns built in sequence

Constructing a wooden arch support

Supervising engineer

Removing waste

Stones

Digging out ditch

Supervising centurion

One of your first jobs will be to improve and extend the roads in your province. Supplies and troops can then move around easily. Your surveyors should plan the road to make it as straight as possible. This will make the road pass over the shortest route. To build the road, dig out a trench and stamp it down. Level it with a layer of sand.

Crane used for lifting building materials

Plastering finished arches

Wooden scaffolding

Worker turning a wheel to power the crane

Workers' huts

Wooden scaffolding

Unloading barge using a crane

Barrels of nails and other supplies brought by barge

Drainage ditch

Stamping down surface

Laying and leveling filled in material

Lining edge

Fill in the ditch with stones and clay. Put slabs along the edge. Finish with a top layer of flat slabs. Stamp these slabs down so they are even and firm. The final surface should curve upward slightly in the middle so that rain will run off to the sides. Dig ditches along the sides of the road to drain water away. Your men should be able to build about 1000 feet of road a day.

Bathhouse and Town House

If you have done your job well, you could be asked to become the provincial governor. This is a position of high status and responsibility. Build yourself a domus, or splendid town house, to show off your importance.

You should also make sure that the town itself has all the comforts of Roman life. There should be an amphitheater and at least one bathhouse. Slaves will serve you in your homes and in public places. You will have brought some slaves with you on the campaign, but you might have to get others from among the local slave population.

Tiled roof

Enclosed garden (peristyle)

High outer walls with no windows

Mosaic floor

Doors to warm room (tepidarium)

Cold plunge pool

A bathhouse

Hypocaust (underfloor heating)

Hot plunge pool

Hot room (caldarium)

Cold water tank

Hot water cylinders

Stoking the fire

Cold room (frigidarium)

Boiler room

Latrines

Changing room

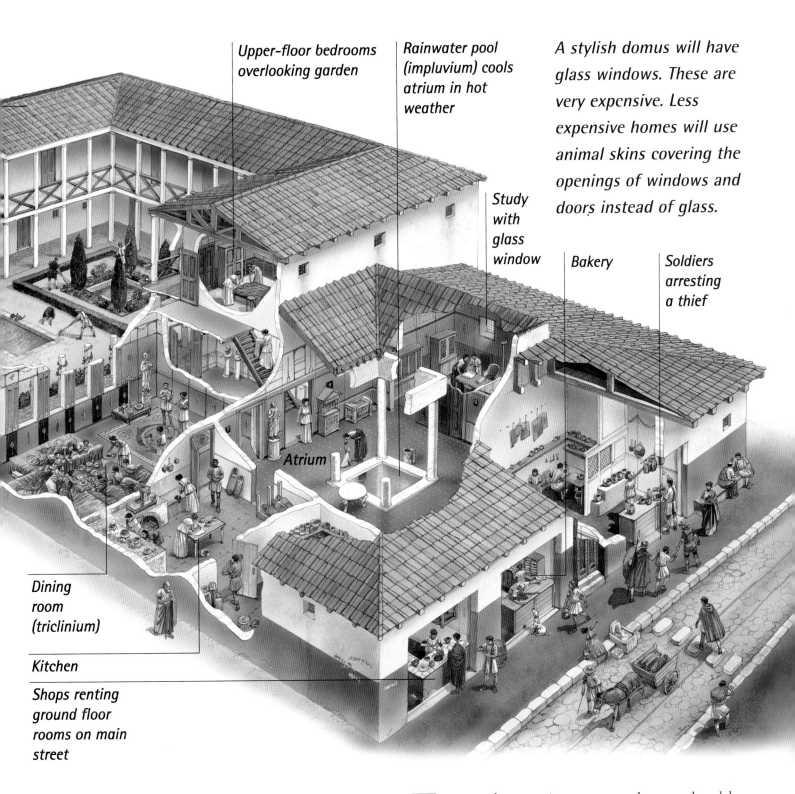

Upper-floor bedrooms overlooking garden

Rainwater pool (impluvium) cools atrium in hot weather

A stylish domus will have glass windows. These are very expensive. Less expensive homes will use animal skins covering the openings of windows and doors instead of glass.

Study with glass window

Bakery

Soldiers arresting a thief

Atrium

Dining room (triclinium)

Kitchen

Shops renting ground floor rooms on main street

Regular bathing in public baths is a Roman custom. Bathhouses are some of the first public buildings you will put up. A furnace in the boiler house heats up the bath water, which is stored in cylinders, as well as the air that moves around under the floors and in the walls. You will need a hypocaust beneath the warm and hot rooms to help keep them heated.

Even in the provinces, your domus should help show local residents who's boss. Impress your guests with a grand central atrium, like a courtyard, with a calming rainwater pool. Mosaics and wall paintings add style. Lower rooms can be rented out as shops. Keep out the noise of the street with high walls and only a few windows and doors around the rest of the house.

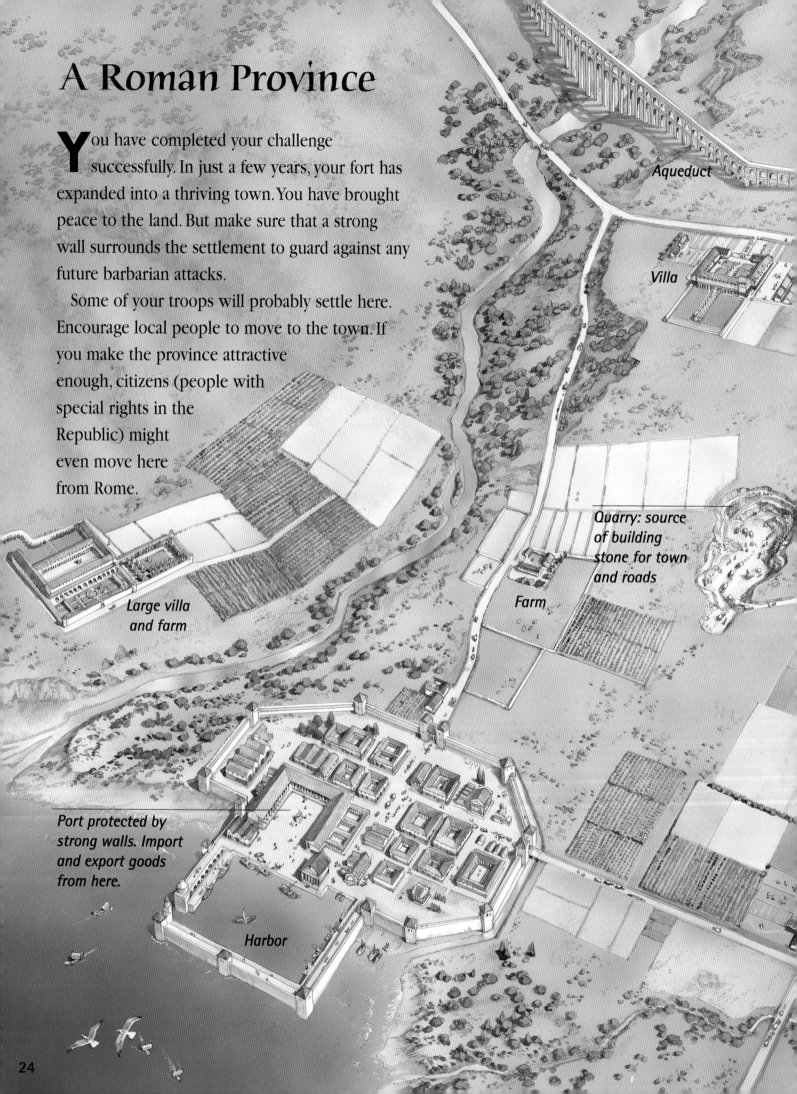

A Roman Province

You have completed your challenge successfully. In just a few years, your fort has expanded into a thriving town. You have brought peace to the land. But make sure that a strong wall surrounds the settlement to guard against any future barbarian attacks.

Some of your troops will probably settle here. Encourage local people to move to the town. If you make the province attractive enough, citizens (people with special rights in the Republic) might even move here from Rome.

Aqueduct

Villa

Quarry: source of building stone for town and roads

Large villa and farm

Farm

Port protected by strong walls. Import and export goods from here.

Harbor

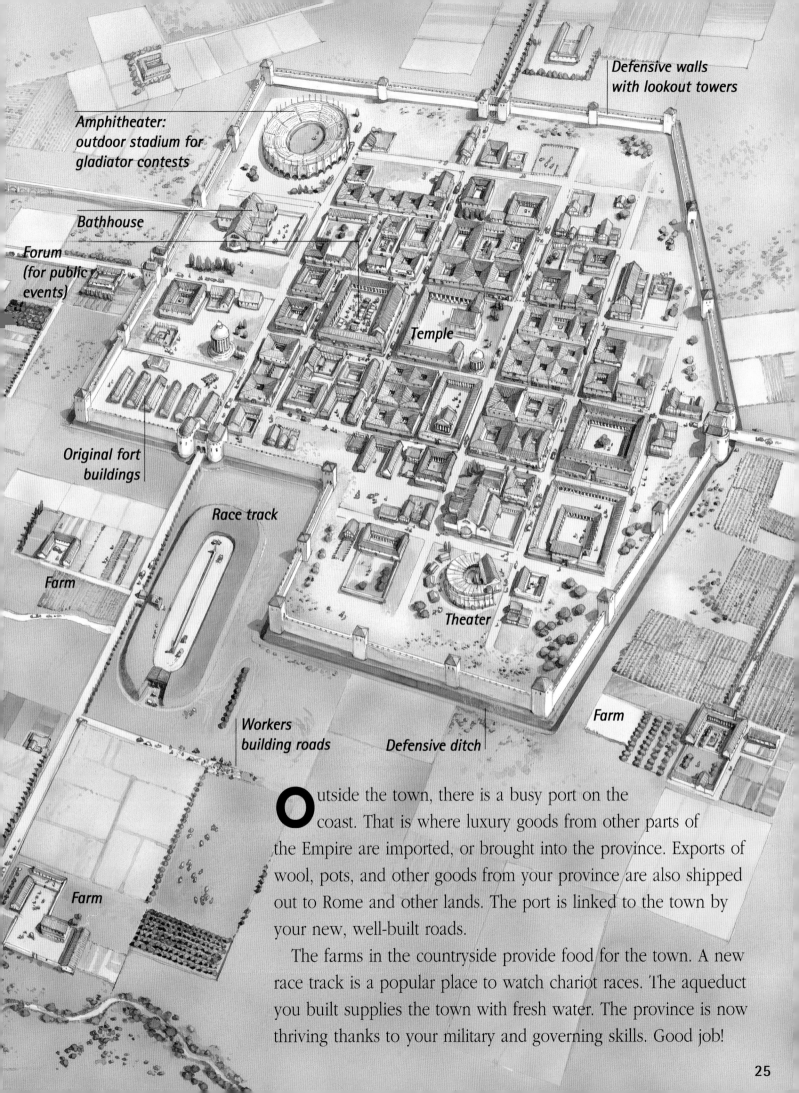

Amphitheater: outdoor stadium for gladiator contests

Bathhouse

Forum (for public events)

Defensive walls with lookout towers

Temple

Original fort buildings

Race track

Farm

Farm

Workers building roads

Defensive ditch

Theater

Farm

Outside the town, there is a busy port on the coast. That is where luxury goods from other parts of the Empire are imported, or brought into the province. Exports of wool, pots, and other goods from your province are also shipped out to Rome and other lands. The port is linked to the town by your new, well-built roads.

The farms in the countryside provide food for the town. A new race track is a popular place to watch chariot races. The aqueduct you built supplies the town with fresh water. The province is now thriving thanks to your military and governing skills. Good job!

Timeline

753 BC

The city of Rome begins to be built in what is now modern Italy.

510 BC

Rome becomes a republic. It is ruled by the Senate, a group of men from wealthy Roman families. Over the next 250 years Rome gradually conquers the country around it.

264 BC

Rome now controls all of Italy. The Punic Wars between Rome and the North African city of Carthage begin. Each side seeks control over the Mediterranean Sea.

218 BC

Hannibal, a Carthaginian general, leads a massive army—including 37 elephants—across the Pyrenees and Alps to invade Italy.

202 BC

Rome defeats Hannibal and invades Spain.

146 BC

Rome conquers Greece.

73–71 BC

Gladiator Spartacus leads a revolt of 90,000 slaves against the Republic. After several victories the revolt is finally put down by the army. Spartacus is killed in battle.

58–51 BC

Julius Caesar, a clever politician and general from a wealthy Roman family, conquers Gaul (France) and becomes popular in Rome.

49 BC

Julius Caesar takes control of Rome, becoming its most powerful leader ever. He brings in new laws to make Rome wealthier.

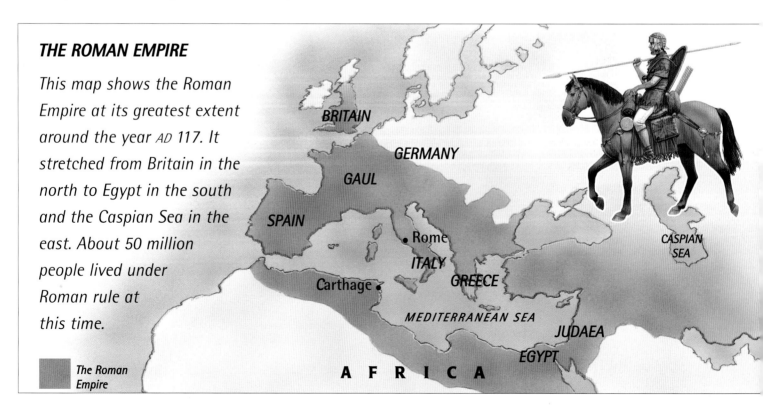

THE ROMAN EMPIRE

This map shows the Roman Empire at its greatest extent around the year AD 117. It stretched from Britain in the north to Egypt in the south and the Caspian Sea in the east. About 50 million people lived under Roman rule at this time.

The Roman Empire

BRITAIN
GERMANY
GAUL
SPAIN
Rome
ITALY
GREECE
Carthage
MEDITERRANEAN SEA
CASPIAN SEA
JUDAEA
EGYPT
A F R I C A

44 BC
Julius Caesar is assassinated by a group of senators, who believe he has become too powerful. A struggle to succeed him follows between Octavian (Caesar's adopted son) and Mark Antony, a Roman general.

31 BC
Octavian defeats Mark Antony, who fought for the Egyptian queen Cleopatra, at the Battle of Actium, Greece. Egypt becomes a Roman province.

27 BC
Octavian becomes the first emperor of Rome, marking the beginning of the Roman Empire. He takes the name Augustus. He dies 41 years later in AD 14.

AD 43
Emperor Claudius, the fourth emperor of Rome, conquers Britain.

AD 60
British leader Boudicca rebels against Roman rule, but is defeated.

AD 105–117
Emperor Trajan conquers land in eastern Europe and the Empire reaches its largest extent.

AD 235–284
Plague, famine, rebellions, and barbarian attacks weaken the Empire. Rome is defeated in the Eastern Empire by Persia in AD 260.

AD 370–410
The Empire is invaded by Huns from Asia and barbarians from the north and east. Romans withdraw from Gaul and Britain.

Boudicca leads a rebellion in Britain in AD 60

AD 395
The Empire is split into two parts, East and West. The Western Empire is soon overrun by barbarians. Rome never again regains its former extent.

AD 410
Rome is sacked by the Goths. Attacks by Vandals in AD 455 further weaken Rome.

AD 476
Barbarian general Odoacer defeats Emperor Romulus Augustulus and makes himself King of Italy, marking the end of the Western Empire.

Vandals destroy Rome in AD 455

Glossary

amphitheater A place where Romans went to watch entertainment. Usually roughly circular or semicircular with the stage in the center and seats on raised steps all around.

aqueduct A system of pipes and channels that brought clean water into towns from natural springs and rivers.

barbarian A person who lived outside the Roman Empire. Barbarians were regarded by the Romans as rough and uncivilized.

basilica A large public building, often built in the town's central square, where important local business was carried out.

centurion Commanding officer of a century.

century Army unit of 80 men.

A Roman chariot race

A centurion shows off his phalerae (medals)

chariot A cart with two wheels pulled by horses. The Romans used chariots for transportation and racing.

citizen A man born in Rome to Roman parents who could vote and serve in the army. In AD 212, all free men were granted citizenship.

cuirass Leather or metal body armor worn by Roman soldiers. It was made of several strips joined together to make it more flexible than a single piece would be.

denarius A silver coin. In the first century AD a legionary was paid 225 denarii a year.

Empire The lands and people controlled by Rome for about 500 years, starting in 27 BC. The Empire was ruled by an emperor.

forum An open space in the middle of a town where markets were held. The forum was also a popular meeting place.

gladiator A slave, criminal, or prisoner of war trained to fight other gladiators and animals in arenas to entertain the people. Gladiators sometimes fought to the death. After many victories gladiators might be given their freedom. Most gladiators were men, though there were also a few women gladiators.

governor The ruler of a Roman province. Sometimes a high-ranking soldier would become governor of a province.

hypocaust A central heating system under floors and walls using hot air from a furnace forced through channels.

Latin The official spoken and written language of the Roman Empire. No longer spoken in everyday life, there are many words of Latin origin in modern European languages, such as English (especially medical and scientific words), French, Italian, and Spanish.

legion The largest unit of the Roman army, made up of around 5000 men.

mosaic A decorative pattern or picture made from colored pieces of stone, pottery, or glass stuck in cement. Mosaics were often used to decorate floors.

phalerae Disc-shaped medals worn by soldiers on leather straps on their chest.

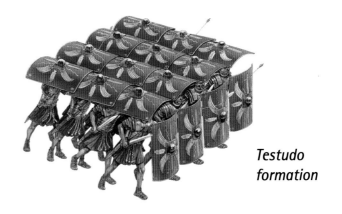

Testudo formation

prima cohort A legion's largest cohort, made up of ten centuries (800 men). Cohorts, or Roman infantry units, were usually six centuries (480 men).

Republic Rome between 509 and 27 BC, ruled by the Senate.

Senate A group of elected men who helped govern both the Republic and the Empire.

slave A person who is bought by another person to work for them for free. Slaves had no rights and were treated like property. They could only be set free by their master.

testudo A military formation in which soldiers arrange their shields to protect the whole group.

Gladiators doing battle

Further Reading

Books

Malam, John. *Ancient Rome.* Chicago, Ill.: Raintree, 2007.

Mulvihill, Margaret. *Roman Forts.* North Mankato, Minn.: Stargazer Books, 2007.

Reece, Katherine. *The Romans: Builders of an Empire.* Vero Beach, Fla.: Rourke Publishing, 2006.

Internet Addresses

Ancient Rome
http://www.historyforkids.org/learn/romans/

The Ancient Romans
http://www.kidspast.com/world-history/0076-ancient-rome.php

The Romans
http://www.bbc.co.uk/schools/romans/

Index